Born Again
A Modernite's Journey

Dedication

This book is dedicated to all the wonderful people who founded this great institution and generations of Life Trustees, Principals, Teachers, Staff and others who nurtured it over 100 years.

Also, to generations of Modernites who created and built voluntary entities like Modern School Old Students Association and The Modernites Trust and developed them as platforms to give back to the alma mater and the communities.

Finally, I dedicate it to my family and friends who supported me in this long journey, which is not over yet.

Born Again
A Modernite's Journey

Sunder Hemrajani

Allied Publishers Pvt. Ltd.
NEW DELHI • MUMBAI • KOLKATA
CHENNAI • BANGALORE • HYDERABAD

ALLIED PUBLISHERS PRIVATE LIMITED

D-5, Sector-2, **Noida**–201 301
Ph. Nos.: 0120-4320295/2542557/4352866 • E-mail: delhi.books@alliedpublishers.com

17 Chittaranjan Avenue, **Kolkata**–700072
Ph.: 033-22129618 • E-mail: cal.books@alliedpublishers.com

15 J.N. Heredia Marg, Ballard Estate, **Mumbai**–400001
Ph.: 022-42126969 • E-mail: mumbai.books@alliedpublishers.com

No. 25/10 Commander-in-Chief Road, Ethiraj Lane (Next to Post Office) Egmore, **Chennai**–600008
Ph.: 044-28223938 • E-mail: chennai.books@alliedpublishers.com

P.B No. 9932, No. 15, 3rd Floor (Next to Vijaya Bank), 5th Cross, Gandhinagar, Karnataka, **Bangalore**–560009
Ph.: 080-41530285 / 22386239
• E-mail: bngl.journals@alliedpublishers.com / apsabng@airtelmail.in

Sri Jayalakshmi Nilayam, No. 3-4-510, 3rd Floor (Above More Super Market) Barkatpura, **Hyderabad**–500027
Ph.: 040-27551811, 040-27551812 • E-mail: hyd.books@alliedpublishers.com

Website: www.alliedpublishers.com

ISBN: 978-93-90951-27-7

Foreword

Sunder has often spoken to me of his memories of years at Modern School, and how his school experiences shaped his personality in so many myriad ways that ultimately influenced almost all of his life's key decisions. A few months ago, he told me that the long covid related lockdowns had propelled him to start documenting his experiences, to record not only his abiding love for his alma mater, but also the lifelong learnings he has attained through his alumni engagements. He felt that documenting his journey with his school could bring out an academic perspective on how school life could shape a personality.

The result is that through his book, Sunder has evocatively captured memories of his childhood, and through his reminiscences, he evokes a time when students led a simpler life without the hustle of pressures that students experience today. With humorous narratives and pictorial representations, he captures the essence of a time when children grew up enjoying small joys and tribulations, without the tearing hurry and competition that students face nowadays.

Through his experiences, Sunder's book also demonstrates that developmental progression in children cannot be rushed. It leads the reader to ponder over the unfiltered exposure to overage content and experiences that children face today, and which engenders confusion and conflicts in their minds as they are unable to process some subjects beyond their developmental age.

An underlying thread throughout his narrative, Sunder has shared how his love of sports and his deeply entrenched value of community engagement and empathy, is a lesson that every school should aspire to. His own experiences are held up as a mirror to showcase how to build an inclusive and caring society.

Ms. Ambika Pant
Honorary Secretary
Board of Trustees
Modern School

Preface

'Pursuing with no less singleness of purpose its (Modern School's) aim is to turn little children into good citizens and honourable gentlemen.'

—'A Successful Experiment in Education'
by Founder Lala Raghubir Singh

'Community Service in an independent fee charging school is essential as it brings the comparatively affluent student in touch with the less fortunate.'

—Principal M.N. Kapur's
49th Founder's Day address in 1969

As I look back over the last 66 years, there have been various events which have shaped my life. The most significant has been my association with Modern School, both as a student and an alumnus. When I trudged into Modern School as a Nursery student in 1959, I did not know the impact the school was going to have on my life. The long association with the alma mater has been a life changing experience. Even today, the school continues to inspire me.

As a Student: The Transformation

I was a reluctant student to start with. The move to the imposing red brick building was a big leap from the neighborhood school I had joined before Modern. Every morning, a walk to the school bus-stop with my grandfather was drudgery I tried to avoid. A move to the new building at Humayun Road in 1961 was a welcome change. The teachers were very kind to the introverted student. As years passed, the sporting activities facilitated the transition from an introvert to a confident child. Academics was not my forte. The playing fields provided me the opportunity to show my talent and hone my skills. I was a member of Hockey, Athletics and Rugger Touch teams. This experience helped me learn my first lessons in Leadership and Teamwork. The school trips to the mountains—Nainital, Dalhousie and Kulu/Manali brought forth my love for mountaineering and trekking. Principal Kapur was an inspiration and a mentor. By the time I graduated from the school, I was ready to take on the challenges ahead. The values of 'Integrity' and 'Respect' imbibed during this phase were precious. ***Integrity* meant there was no right way to do a wrong thing. *Respect* entails you should treat others as you would like to be treated.**

As an Alumnus: Serving the Alma Mater

I continued to build on the foundation during my years in the engineering college and management school. The lessons of Modern were never forgotten. One had to be a good human being to succeed as a professional. My second innings with Modern started when I was posted in Delhi by Hindustan Unilever Ltd (HUL), my employer. I got involved in the activities organized by Modern School Old Students Association (MSOSA) for the Platinum Jubilee celebrations of the school. My journey to support and serve my alma mater had just begun.

I was elected to the Executive Committee of MSOSA in 1995 and was its President from 1998–2000. During this stint, MSOSA undertook the project of renovation of the old gym (MN Kapur Hall) and executed it to perfection with funds (Rs 27 lacs) raised through activities and donations from Modernites. Nomination to the Managing Committee (MC) of Modern School, Barakhamba Road (BKR) followed in 2002. I was also asked to conduct Vision-Mission workshops in all the three schools and undertook an assignment (Project Everest) on behalf of the MC to devise a roadmap to raise the bar and promote excellence in the school. Served on the MC of Modern Vasant Vihar from 2011–14 and rejoined the MC of Modern BKR in 2014.

I was nominated to The Modernites Trust by MSOSA in 1996. Subsequently, I was nominated as a Permanent Trustee and was selected by the Trustees as the Chairman of the Trust in 2008. Since then, the Trust has expanded the scope of the Scholarship and Gurudakshina programs. I was nominated as a Term Trustee by the Modern School Board of Trustees (BOT) in 2019 and was elected as the President of MSOSA in 2020. I am also associated with the Institute for Research and Development in School Education (IRDSE) undertaken by the BOT to celebrate the centenary of Modern School.

Looking back at my second innings, I have been privileged to be offered platforms like MSOSA, The Modernites Trust, Managing Committee, and the BOT to serve the school at various levels. Serving the various internal stakeholders—students, staff, alumni fraternity and the community outside has made this journey fruitful and worthwhile. This journey is not over yet. I will cherish this long association forever.

This book is an attempt to cover both innings—as a student and as an alumnus. The reader should find it interesting and hopefully be motivated to seek happiness and fulfillment through serving the community

It is said 'You can take the student out of Modern but never Modern out of the student'.

Sunder Hemrajani
Modernite, Class of '72

Prayer

"You are what your deepest desire is.
As your desire is, so is your intention.
As your intention is, so is your will.
As your will is, so is you deed.
As your deed is, so is your destiny."

—Brihadaranyaka Upanishad

Acknowledgement

Modern School celebrated its centenary in 2020. It was a significant milestone in the history of this great institution. Its history and the contribution to nation building is chronicled in various books written on the subject, starting with the book by its Founder Late Lala Raghubir Singh titled 'A Successful Experiment in Education', co-authored with first Principal of the school Late Ms. Kamala Bose. The second book on Modern School released during the Platinum Jubilee celebrations was the iconic 'A Dream Turns Seventy-Five' co-authored by eminent Modernites Late Mr. Khushwant Singh and Dr. Syeda Hameed. The latest book 'The Modern School (1920–2020): A Century of Schooling in India' authored by Prof. Rakesh Batabyal chronicled the journey of the school over 100 years. I have read all the 3 books and they have given me insights into the vision of the founder and the progress the school made to realize his vision during different eras. This knowledge has also impacted me personally and enabled me to navigate the journey.

I have had a close engagement with several Life Trustees in the last 30 years. Their trust and affection have been quite motivating especially the past Presidents Late Major General Virendra Singh (Retd), Mr. Ashok Pratap Singh, Ms. Ketaki Sood, Ms. Anuradha Pratap Singh and the gen-next represented by Late Mr. Pradeep Virendra Singh, Ms. Mira Pradeep Singh and Ms. Ambika Pant. I am grateful to Ms. Ambika Pant, Honorary Secretary, Board of Trustees, Modern School for writing the foreword for this book. She has been a constant source of encouragement. I also value the contribution of Dr. Vijay Datta, the current Principal of

Modern School, Barakhamba Road whose quote mentioned on the front cover of the book helped me structure my thoughts.

I am grateful to my friend and classmate from Modern, Class of '72 Mr. Ravi Sachdev and his committed team of Chief Consulting Editor Mr. Sharad Gupta and Editor Mr. Jagdish Singh. The contribution of Mr. Sunil Handoo is priceless. He provided wonderful illustrations which brought various anecdotes in the book to life.

Finally, I must express my gratitude to my wonderful family, my wife Kamala and sons Akhil (Class of 2005) and Rohan (Class of 2007) who have been a constant source of encouragement in this journey.

Contents

1st Innings

2nd Innings

1st Innings

1

Prelude—The Admission Drama

This is an important piece to write since it provides context to what was to follow. We were living in Old Rajendra Nagar. Our family had relocated from Sindh during partition. The small houses were allotted by the government to refugees as a compensation for what they had left behind. We had 2 houses in the colony. My grandparents used to live in a one room house and my parents and children used to live in a 2-room accommodation allotted to my uncle (Father's elder brother) who was away to London on an official posting as an education counsellor in Indian High Commission. At the age of 3 years, I was admitted by my father into a Montessori School in the neighborhood. The school *ayah* would come in the morning to pick up the children and herd them to the school and drop them back around lunchtime. It was fun because all my friends in the block went to the same school. All that you did there was learn poems, draw images, alphabets, etc.

All this changed in 1959 when my uncle returned from London. He felt that I should join Modern School since it had a very good reputation and being an educationist himself, he had developed great admiration for Principal Kapur who he had interacted with in his role in the government.

I was very reluctant to leave all my friends behind. However, he motivated me to go and see the school and have an interaction with the Principal. So I left with my father on a bus to Connaught Place and took a *phatphatee* (4-seater motorcycle) to the school. As I walked with my father to the massive structure of the school, there was a sense of unease and the effect of the motivational talk evaporated quickly. From a school located in a small bungalow to this imposing structure was a huge leap. It was beyond my imagination. My

The Admission Drama on the Front Porch

father asked me to wait on the gravel path outside the office and went inside to meet Mr. Kapur. I kept looking at the structure and wondered how I will survive my fate. Only silver lining was the swings and slides in the lawn 50 metres away. After a brief period, I saw my father calling out to me from inside the corridor. He was asking me to come inside to meet the Principal. I froze. I suddenly didn't want any of this. I just sat down on the gravel and refused to move. My father was concerned at the sudden turn of events. He walked quickly to take me inside. I resisted with all my might. He started to drag me towards the Principal's office. There was some commotion and suddenly I saw the imposing personality of a tall man walking towards us. This had to be Principal Kapur. He told my father who by now had gone red with fury to leave me. My father thought I had blown it. The Principal asked me if I wanted to play on the swings. I was speechless and just nodded my head. He said go and play. I ran towards the swing as fast as I could. I had to get out of my father's reach as soon as possible. While I was playing, Mr Kapur told my anxious father that the admission was granted, and he could send me to school the next day in school bus.

Even today, I wonder why I got the admission in the school. Maybe, Mr. Kapur was impressed with the speed at which I ran towards the swings. A future athlete in the making?

2

Modern School— A Reluctant Beginning

While the family was relieved when the admission was granted, they were still concerned about my reaction. I didn't seem too excited. Next day, when I was woken up early to catch the school bus, my grandmother kept me in good humor by giving me some toffees. My father undertook the difficult task of taking me to the bus-stop which was about 300 metres away. I was

Granny's Incentive for Attending the School

A Special Relationship with Grandfather

extremely reluctant and hence started resisting. The last resort was to cry which I did. But to no avail. My father was equally determined to put me on the bus. The events of the previous day had hardened him. My last stand was at the bus-stop where I refused to get into the bus. The bus monitor's help was sought, and I found myself taking a ride to the school after some pull and push during boarding.

The ride to the school was uneventful. I spent the day with friendly teachers who were very considerate, took care of the new student. During the break, the *ayah* took me to the place where sweetened milk was kept for consumption by the students. My mother had packed a sandwich. I wandered around the playgrounds and went back to the class when the bell rang. I was relieved when the classes were over, and took bus ride back home. I was welcomed at the bus stop by my grandfather who walked me home. My grandfather was very

A Reluctant Walk to School Bus-stop with Grandfather

fond of me. He showered me with love and affection, supplemented by a pocket money of one anna per week from his meagre pension.

He undertook the responsibility of walking me to the bus stop in the morning and picking me up on return. The family realized that I had a special relationship with him. This was fully leveraged to perform the difficult task of putting me on the school bus.

I settled down quickly. I also made some friends in my section ('A' section). My first two years in the school were happy years. My grandfather played the role of my mentor to the hilt. When we shifted our residence to Netaji Nagar in 1961, he continued to drop me at the bus-stop 2 km away at Laxmibai Nagar on his cycle and would pick me on return. Our servant would fill in whenever he couldn't make it.

3

National Defence Fund Effort

There was a massive fundraising effort post the Indo-China war in 1962. The school also decided to contribute its might. The reason I remember this is because it had a huge impact on my psyche. Life was not about oneself but there was a bigger purpose. You must think beyond yourself—country and community were important. These were my formative years.

Mrs. Uma Sahay—The Final Appeal for Funds

Our class teacher was Mrs. Uma Sahay. She was a strict teacher but with a kind heart. She appealed for fund collection. Everyone was requested to contribute whatever they could. I went home and told my father about the initiative. He agreed to do so. Our class was the highest contributor in the KG School, but we were short of the magical figure of Rs 1000. There was one more day to go before the deadline. Mrs. Sahay walked into the class looking very serious and announced that we were short of the target by approx. Rs 100. She made an emotional appeal with breaking voice, requesting for some more contribution. She also said that if we turn up short of the target, she will start crying, *'Mein ro padungi'* (I will start crying) was the ultimate refrain. I remember going back to my father asking for more which he readily agreed. The next day most of the children brought in more and the class exceeded the target by a significant amount. Mrs. Sahay was all smiles and thanked the whole class.

This is an experience which I cherish after more than 50 years, my first effort for charity.

4

The Milk Break

I was at the Junior School (RSJMS) from 1961–67 (KG3-J4). The Milk Break was an important part of the school timetable. Every student was required to drink a small bottle of milk every day. Students who were lactose intolerant were

Drinking Milk was Compulsory

exempt, a packet of glucose biscuits was an option. A letter from the parent was necessary for exemption. We were expected to queue up in the school courtyard for the daily dose of sweetened milk supplied by Delhi Milk Scheme (DMS) in small bottles. This was compulsory. To ensure no one escaped, the class captain kept track with the attendance sheet. The absentees were called in for explanation. Many years later, it was replaced with a non-sweetened variant. Some students used to carry Bournvita to the school in small packets to make it palatable.

After tanking up, the children freaked out on the field, playing innovative games like hand cricket, hand tennis and king-queen, all played with great gusto with a tennis ball. The bell, signaling the end of the break, was a sound one didn't want to hear. The Milk Break was the most enjoyable part of the day.

In the Senior School (Modern BKR), the Milk Break continued to be a part of the timetable but there was a difference. It was no longer compulsory to drink milk. Since it was a full day school, a Lunch Break was included in the timetable.

5

My Housemaster and Me

In the junior school, I was in Dayanand House. My housemaster was Mr Ram Singh, a multi-talented person. Apart from teaching Hindi, he also acted in plays. He played the role of legendry warrior Porus. He had a booming voice which did full justice to his tough personality. He was a strict disciplinarian, a key trait for a housemaster. The house-master was supposed to play a role of a parent and counsellor inside the school. If you had any problem, academic or otherwise, you could approach the housemaster.

Mr. Ram Singh on the Morning Grooming Check

There was a system in the school where a housemaster would check the grooming of the wards. Polished shoes, short nails and short hair was a norm. When the day started, all students queued up by their house for the check.

I was fond of playing hand-cricket with my classmates in the morning. It was played with hand instead of a bat and tennis ball with the sideboard of the hockey goalpost as wicket. It was a popular game and players used to reach early in the morning to play the game. The dew was a problem in winter. The shoes used to be covered with grass, mud and dew. When bell rang, the players used to run to join the queue and, on the way, clean the shoes with whatever one could find. Once, I didn't clean the shoes properly since scoring the winning run was more important. I went and stood in the queue waiting for the check to start. Mr. Ram Singh started the check from one end looking at each student from shoes to the head. He came and stood opposite me. His gaze stuck on my shoes and smack... the *thappad* found my face. He threatened to give me a yellow card if it was repeated. That was the end of a budding cricketing career and Sunil Gavaskar got lucky.

I would like to point out that since that day, I always polish my shoes before leaving home. It was a lesson learnt for life.

6

My Tryst with Hand Tennis

Since the hand cricket episode in my life ended in a *thappad*, new avenues had to be found for channelizing the energy in the morning. It couldn't be on the lawn. The concrete floor in the courtyard, outside the craft room was an attractive option. The creative genius of the wards enabled them to come up with hand tennis in the small patch between the two entrances to the room. There was a minor risk of hitting the glass window, but the players were confident that the challenge could be overcome. This game was played with hand and tennis ball. Since the number of players was large, only doubles were played. It took off very well. The boys enjoyed the game. No danger of spoiling the shine on the shoes. This carried on for days and months till one of the players decided to try a spin serve. It's not easy to spin while serving with a racquet, spinning with hand was not even worth trying. Instead of hitting the floor on the opposite side, the ball took a different trajectory and hit the window glass with a great force and cracked it up. The players left the improvised court and dissolved in the crowd. It signaled that the last game of hand tennis had been played. The promising careers came to a premature end and Vijay Amritraj got a walkover.

The students transitioned to hand squash. More about it later.

Hand Tennis—The Spin Serve

7

AKC—My Teacher, My Coach

As I grew up in school, there were several people who influenced me. They shaped my character and my values. I was raised in a joint family. At home, my uncle spent a lot of time and effort on my upbringing. In the school, Mr. AK Chaturvedi (AKC), our Hindi teacher and a hockey coach was amongst the few who helped me grow from an introvert to a confident child. My first exposure to him was on the hockey field in junior school. Those days, a student was exposed to all the games during the games period. This enabled one to make a choice regarding the game one wanted to pursue later in school. Unlike other coaches, AKC used to pick up the hockey stick and play with us on the field. He was an active hockey player who played in the Delhi Hockey League for the New Stars Club. I remember once I had scored 2 goals during the game. AKC had the ball and could have easily scored the goal himself. He called out to me and passed the ball to me to help me complete a hat trick. He was a wonderful human being whose kindness touched the lives of many students in the school. His antics during the annual staff *vs* students cricket match had everyone in splits.

My association with AKC continued in the senior school (S1-S5) since I played hockey throughout my tenure there. The relationship with him and his family continued even after school. This is a relationship which I would cherish forever.

With AKC on the Hockey Field

8

Changing the Mindset

I moved to junior school in J1 (Class 3) in 1963. I was not interested in academics. I wouldn't concentrate in the classroom and was not bothered about homework. This is the period in which I received two white chits for my repeated acts of omission.

A third white chit would have possibly led to a yellow card, a higher-level punishment which was given in the morning assembly. This would have also come to the notice of my strict housemaster Mr. Ram Singh. This somewhat changed my attitude from 'no interest' in academics to doing the 'bare minimum'. I struggled with all the subjects. Even poor performance in terminal and half yearly exams didn't encourage me to work harder. I would appear for exams without any preparation. I barely managed to pass.

My father was not amused. It was in J3 that my fortunes changed. My uncle who started his career as a teacher took charge and ensured I spent one hour with him every evening. Weekend sessions could last up to 2 hours. Also, introduction of General Knowledge (GK) as the subject helped. I used to read the daily newspaper (The Statesman) and Illustrated Weekly of India. My GK was pretty good. My scores improved and I started clocking 65-90% in various subjects. This was a turning point.

All along in junior school, sports were a priority. I played games like football and cricket at home and in school. This was the phase when I also discovered an athlete in me. I could run fast.

Move to senior school accelerated the change in me. My housemaster CK Chadha took interest in my development. Small successes in academics and sports spurred me on. Mr. AK Chaturvedi's (AKC) return to senior school also helped. I joined the school hockey team. Head of Sports, Mr. LN Khurana encouraged me to join athletics and rugger touch teams. The introverted child had transformed into a confident teenager. The Principal Mr. Kapur told my uncle on the last day in the school, 'Mr. Hemrajani, Sunder has shaped up very well. He will do well in life. You don't have to worry about him.' These words have stayed with me since then. Whenever I have self-doubts, I remember them.

Being Counselled for Poor Marks

9

A Trip to Nainital

Your schooldays cannot be complete without a few school trips with your classmates. These are different experiences under different conditions. There are no pressures of homework and classroom supervision. Even the staff members who accompany you are more relaxed, and the younger ones are more like your friends as long as you don't cross a line.

There were 3 trips announced for that summer vacation—Mussoorie, Mount Abu and Nainital. I signed up for Nainital. It was a big group of approx. 80–90 students from J3 & J4 classes in the junior school. The teachers who escorted us were led by a strict Mr. HL Batra, our Maths teacher. Then we had the young ones like Ms. Neena Ghei, Mr. BC Sharma, the Dance teacher, and Ms. Lee, who was in our school as a part of the teacher exchange program. We crowded into the 3rd Class Sleeper bogie of Indian Railways. Packed dinner was served on the train. We found ourselves at Moradabad Station in the morning after an uneventful journey. We were then herded into a bus after a quick breakfast and then on the road to Nainital. I was sitting right in front of the bus on the single seat next to the driver. Given that I didn't sleep well in the train, I kept dozing off. I didn't realize then that the person in that seat is not supposed to sleep since it can make the driver sleepy. Neena Ghei woke me up and branded me a 'Sleepy Head' for the rest of the trip. Thankfully, the name didn't stick back in the school.

We reached Nainital in the evening and stayed at Elphinstone Hotel which was quite central. We retired into our respective dorms after dinner. Next day, we went around Nainital basically enjoying the walk around Naini Lake and did a bit of shopping. The adventurous ones made it to the skating rink. Much of the time there was spent in visiting the tourist spots—Land's End, Dorothy's Seat, Tiffin Top and Snow View. We also walked to Cheena Peak at a height of 8000 ft. It was an arduous walk. After a brief rest, we walked back to the hotel. We undertook a one-day trip to Bhimtal and Naukuchiatal. Throwing flat stones on the placid surface at Naukuchiatal was a fascinating experience. Another memorable experience

Skating in Nainital

was watching a Shammi Kapoor movie *Teesri Manzil* which was released that week. Everyone was given a choice of watching *Teesri Manzil* or *Sagaai*. While all the girls in the group opted for *Sagaai*, all the boys except one chose *Teesri Manzil*. That brave heart was Virat Kohli of our school team Bhuvnesh Chadha. He escorted the girls to *Sagaai*. Even today *Teesri Manzil* is my favorite movie.

It was an eventful trip in many ways. It was my first trip without my parents. My love for mountains and trekking started in Nainital in the summer of '67.

Teesri Manzil in Nainital

10

Full Day School—Work and Play

We moved from the junior school at Humayun Road to the senior school in S1 (Class 7) at Barakhamba Road. The first change we observed was that this was a full day school. The day started with the morning assembly with a prayer and the Principal Mr. MN Kapur making announcements and sharing words of wisdom with the students. There were only 600 students in the senior school from S1 to S5. The campus was approx. 27 acres. It was a pleasure walking on gravel covered paths surrounded by greenery. Eucalyptus trees provided the lighter shades of green.

The classes started at 8.30 am and finished at 3.30 pm. The day included 2 breaks—Milk Break and Lunch Break. Milk was optional and available in abundance. Most students carried lunch box from home. The day ended with a sports period followed by an evening assembly when the attendance was taken to ensure no one skipped sports. Mr. Kapur himself would walkabout to see that every student participated in some game. If he found someone loitering around, he would personally escort the defaulter to the game of his choice.

The school was a fun place. Even after school timetable ended, the members of the school teams would stay back to practice. Since I was a member of the school hockey team, I had the pleasure of being coached by AKC who used to play with us.

It was usually a long day but quite enjoyable. Sadly, the full day school was discontinued sometime in the 80s. It's now history.

A Busy Full Day in School

11

Kulu Manali—Watching the Shoot

I was now hooked to the school trips. Any trip to the hill station was something to look forward to. Kulu Manali beckoned in the summer of 1968. This trip was undertaken with the seniors. We set out for the trip with an overnight train journey from New Delhi Railway Station. We reached Chandigarh in the morning and then spent one night there in the guest house. On the cards was a movie at a nearby theatre. Next morning, after breakfast we got into the buses for Kulu. It was a long journey which took us through Bilaspur and Sunder Nagar along the Beas River to the town of Kulu located on the banks of river Beas. The plan was to spend one day there. Some of us climbed a nearby hill. We left for Manali next morning. The valley, surrounded by snowcapped mountains was beautiful. A small hotel in the main *bazar* was to be our abode during our stay there.

There were two significant events on the trip. When we reached Manali, our sightseeing agenda had to undergo a revision. We found out that a movie *Ek Phool Do Mali* was being shot in Manali. So time was created in the schedule to watch the shoot. On day one, after a trek to Sulphur springs at Vashisth, we headed to a bungalow on the other bank of Beas. There we saw a scene of the beggar and a small kid singing a song outside the gate. There was the veteran Balraj Sahni, handsome new actor Sanjay Khan and beautiful Sadhana. In between shots, we got a chance to interact with the stars. The girls in the group obviously focused on Sanjay.

Suddenly, the priorities of the group changed. Next day, the group wanted to see the shoot again. Some action sequences were on the cards. The eager beavers arrived at a different location. There was a sequence where Sadhana is running on the hilly road chased by the beefy villain (Shyam Kumar) when suddenly the hero Sanjay Khan emerges from nowhere, jumps from a hillock and takes on the villain, pushing him to the ground. The shot was canned after a couple of rehearsals.

With Star Sanjay Khan at a Location in Manali

There was one more incident which sticks in the memory. Dr. Baweja who was then a young basketball coach escorted the group on the trip. He and some senior students went out for a morning walk carrying one sling bag. When we went down

On the School Trip—
Stealing Apples in Manali

The Great Escape—
Jumping the Orchard Wall in Manali

a bit later on the same path, we saw Dr. Baweja running with bagful of apples followed by the students. Something was clearly amiss. As the story goes, they had gone to pick some apples from the trees in the nearby orchard. While the boys climbed the boundary wall and undertook the dangerous task of picking the apples, Dr. Baweja stood outside catching the apples thrown to him and filling up the sling bag. Suddenly there was a barking sound and the caretaker with a *lathi*, and his dog started running towards the boys. The boys just about avoided the dog snapping at the heals and jumped over the wall breaking a few athletics records. However, Dr. Baweja who had all the goodies was the fastest in the group. He had to protect the precious cargo.

The rest of the trip was quite uneventful, and we got back to Delhi after a long and tiring journey.

12

Inter School—Play to Finish

I played hockey for the school team for 3 years. There are some incidents which remain etched in my memory even after almost 50 years. In the year 1968, we played the final of the Inter School Junior Hockey tournament which was played against MC Rouse Avenue on the hockey field outside National Stadium.

It was a tough match, and both the teams couldn't score till the final whistle. This was followed by extra time of 30 minutes. Even then there was no goal to separate the two teams. There were no penalty shootouts then. So, what followed was 'Play to finish' which meant you kept playing till someone scored. Both the teams had got tired after more than 100 minutes of the game. The game ended with a goal scored by the player from the opposite side with his foot which was clearly a foul which the referee did not see because of the crowd in front of the goal. The ball which came from outside the circle was stopped by our star goalkeeper Ajay Gupta. It hit the opposing forward on his foot and went into the goal. It was clearly a foul. The referee blew the whistle for the goal and ended the game even before we could register our protest on the field.

It was a disappointing end to a tough game. None of the players spoke for 20 minutes. Our coach, AKC and Head of Sports, Mr. LN Khurana consoled us with words of encouragement, but no one could accept the unfair loss. Even today, that match is etched in my mind.

Playing to the Finish—A Tough Match

13

Breaking a Barrier—Recitation Competition

The school had a vibrant cultural and extra-curricular calendar. This included various school and house events. Given my introverted nature, I was reluctant to participate in these events. The closest I came to getting involved was being a part of the group song during my house function in junior school. I stayed clear of the inter house competitions except in sports.

One day, this peace was broken by my house captain in S3 (Class 9) Guneet Rana, who under instructions of the Housemaster Mr. CK Chadha, told me to participate in the Inter House Hindi Recitation Competition. I tried to argue my case for not participating but could not convince anyone. That was a stressful day. I returned home and told my father about my predicament and asked him if I could take sick leave and if he could give me a letter which I will send to the school through a schoolmate in the neighborhood. He was horrified and said he will not give me any letter and encouraged me to participate. Since I had exhausted all options, I took out my school Hindi textbook to find an easy poem to recite. The poem was called '*Viplav Gaan*'.

Next day, I was second in the queue after Akbar House. I had not memorized the poem and carried a paper on which I had written it. I almost stumbled while getting on the stage. The recitation went alright, and I was delighted to get away from the stage. I subsequently found out that there were 6

Sunder on the Stage—Reciting in the Morning Assembly

participants (out of 12) who recited '*Viplav Gaan*'. Needless to say, the prize winners were amongst the other 6.

This episode helped me come out of my shcll. It was a significant moment in my journey out of introversion.

14

The *Thappad* Era

I spent 13 years of my life in Modern School. These were my formative years. The lessons I learnt during that time hold me in good stead today. There were various procedures used by the school and the teachers to ensure that the young

The *Thappad* Era

wards knew the dos and don'ts. At the institutional level, there were the Good Chits, Yellow Cards and White Cards. At the teacher level, apart from these instruments, there was a *Thappad*, a slap on the face to send a message to the student crossing the line. If the violation was repeated, the *Murga* punishment was resorted to by some. *Murga* as the name suggests was like a cock posture where the student was made to take the arms below the legs in a sit-down mode and hold both the ears. It was inflicted for a short period, normally 5-10 minutes. But the most effective with guaranteed results in short term was a *thappad*. The purpose of the *thappad* was to correct, not to hurt. That's why the hand followed a 30–45-degree arc before it made the contact with the face. Over 95 percent *thappads* were in this category. However, if you upset the teacher by repeated violations, you could expect a *thappad* with a 120–180-degree arc. There were some other more painful methods too. There was a teacher in junior school who would sometimes walk into the class with a cane under his armpit. The signal to the class was clear. There were rumours that he used to bring the cane when he had some disagreements at home and was in a mood to take out his angst. Since the cane signalled the intent, there would be pin drop silence in the class. However, since the teacher was keen to get going, he would then enquire about the homework. He had his favourites who happened to sit on the front corner table. He knew the regular defaulters. He would menacingly approach that table expecting to find his targets. Obviously, the cane used to fly.

There is an interesting episode pertaining to the senior school. Mr Jankidass, our librarian, and boarding house master was very adapt at the *thappads*. After all, he had long years of experience in correcting the naughty boarders.

He was also a chain smoker who would walk down the corridor to the boarding house for a quick puff. His fingers always used to smell of tobacco. He was very strict. In the library, he enforced the no noise rule without any dilution. Once, he found a student talking. He called him out and gave him a tight *thappad* on his face. It left the finger imprint along with the tobacco smell. The student after the class went down the stairs and found MNK in the howler. As he walked past MNK, he was called back because MNK got a whiff of the smell. He asked him if he had been smoking. Before he could respond, he got a *thappad*. The irony was that this student was a non-smoker.

15

Summer of '69—Dalhousie and Beyond

Summer of '69 was upon us and I was ready to go for another trip to the mountains. My love for mountains was kindled during the first school trip to Nainital in 1967, it got reinforced during the trip to Kulu-Manali in 1968. I was now looking forward to my next trip. I signed up for Dalhousie along with my other classmates.

The trip started with an overnight train journey to Pathankot from where we got into buses on a hilly terrain to Dalhousie. Our accommodation was fixed at the Dalhousie Club which was right next to the bus station. Our lunch was organized at a *dhaba* at the bus station called Lal Dhaba. It was a fixed price meal, a thali at a negotiated price of Rs 1.25. This included unlimited quantity of *sabzi*, *dal*, curd and *rotis*. I was a poor eater and didn't do justice to the price but there were a few who made up, especially my hockey team-mate Rohit Mohan Choudhary. Rohit was at home in Dalhousie because he had stayed there earlier, and his sister was studying at a local catholic school. He had an awesome appetite. While some of us would wind up after 2 *tandoori rotis*, Rohit will have at least 6-8 and ask for more. On one occasion he made the *dhaba* owner knead fresh dough for extra *rotis*. The result was that from the next day, the rate went up to Rs 1.75 per *thali*. This increase also encouraged Rohit to up his intake to the dismay of the *dhaba* owner.

A couple of days were spent in trekking to tourist spots in Dalhousie. Satdhara was one of them. After spending a few days in Dalhousie, we commenced a 12 km trek to a scenic meadow surrounded by pine trees called Khajjiar. It was a beautiful place. We rested for the night in the cottages available there and next day were ready for a 14 km trek to

Trekking around Dalhousie

the district headquarter town of Chamba. On the way, we took shortcuts through farm terraces to reach Chamba after crossing a bridge on the turbulent river Chenab.

The second leg of the school trip started with a bus ride to Katra located at the foot of Trikuta Hills. This small town was also a starting point for a trek to the temple of Mata Vaishno Devi. There was 10 km trek from Katra to the temple. We started in the afternoon. The track was uneven and rocky, and the progress was slow. Darkness slowed us down further. The torch batteries also were considerably weakened. We hitched ourselves to the group of BSF jawans whom we befriended at a tea *dhaba* enroute. They were friendly and gave us advise on how to deal with the treacherous mule track at night. We gave a pass to the Bhairon temple at night and proceeded quickly to the main temple.

We reached there close to midnight and had *darshan* after a cold shower out in the open. To get to the inner cave where the idols were, one had to crawl through a small hole in the outer cave formation. The accommodation assigned to us was already occupied by a family and we had to make do with an uncomfortable hard place on the open terrace. We were all tired after a hard trek which helped us sleep through whatever was left of the night. The next morning, we left for our base at Katra after breakfast.

The journey from Katra to Delhi via Pathankot was quite uneventful. Overall, the trip was quite enjoyable though a bit tiring. It also reinforced my love for the mountains.

16

NCC Camps in the Mountains

National Cadet Corps (NCC) was started as a program with the motto 'Unity and Discipline' by the government to make up the shortfall in the defence forces in case of emergencies. This was broadly a 2 year program covering classes 9 (S3) and 10 (S4). Apart from the weekly drills in the school, the trained cadre gave a Guard of Honor to the Chief Guest on the school's Annual Founders Day. The high point however was the NCC camp held at the end of the year.

In the first year of our program, the NCC camp was organized in Bhowali, a small hamlet near Nainital in the Kumaon Hills. It was situated at an elevation of 1600 metres, 11 km from Nainital. The travel was by train to Kathgodam and then by Army trucks to the camp site. Eight cadets were assigned to each tent. The day started with morning tea followed by a run and physical exercises. There was a session to learn shooting where you were taught to handle a rifle and fire at targets consisting of concentric circles located 25 metres away. You were taken to the surrounding hills for walks and knowledge sessions. It was tough but interesting. During short breaks, the cadets were encouraged to sing or act. Our classmate Arun Kuckreja performed a memorable act of Shammi Kapoor's 'Yahoo' song from Bollywood film *Kashmir ki Kali* by rolling down the hill. The food was average, but the hungry cadets used to have it without any complaints. The route march to Nainital was tough but enjoyable.

The Yahoo Song on the Slopes

The second camp a year later was held at Neugal Khud, a place near the district headquarters of Palampur, Himachal Pradesh. It was a very scenic site with the view of the majestic

Dhauladhar range of mountains in Himalayas. We were asked to pitch the tents on the beautiful green meadows. The tent was surrounded by a pit to keep the reptiles out. The first evening itself, there was heavy rain and the pit helped keep the water out. The physical training (PT) sessions which included runs on the road surrounded by tea gardens were grueling but enjoyable. A small gushing stream of water running through the meadows provided a spot for a refreshing bath. A group of cadets attempted a sneak trip to Palampur late in the night through the tea gardens but turned back due to the barking of ferocious dogs and sounds of other wild animals. A day trip to Dharamsala was also on the cards. A briefing session organized on the ammunition used in warfare was interesting.

The camps served the purpose of training the cadets for a role during emergencies. It was also a platform which offered a glimpse of army life in the school for cadets to opt for a career in the defence forces later.

17

The Chalk Wars

I grew up in an era when the blackboards and chalk were the favorite tools for a teacher. There were many teachers who preferred to read from the text books and explain the subject like languages (Hindi, English, Sanskrit) and Social Studies to the students, but there were many who would happily go to the blackboard and write with the chalk to make their point. This was especially true of the sciences (Physics, Chemistry, Biology) and Mathematics.

When you walked into the classroom, a box of chalks with a duster was always kept in one corner of the board. The chalks also came in handy for some naughty students in the class to trouble their fellow students. I have been a witness to many chalk wars in the classroom but I participated in one which has stuck in my memory.

Once the teacher who was supposed to take the class was absent and our Head of Sports, Mr. LN Khurana (LNK) was requested to stand in for her. I think it was Mrs. Sudha Shivpuri who used to teach us Hindi. She normally took classes in the room right opposite Principal Mr. Kapur's office which was supposed to be a silent zone. LNK walked in and told us to study any subject and warned us not to make any noise since the Principal was in his office. I happened to be sitting in the last row, my favorite place along with my close friend Rajnish Kataria who was known for his naughty behavior. He suddenly found a full box of chalks in the storage section of the desk. He took out the chalks and broke them into various pieces. The front row was occupied by the academic toppers. He aimed one at Vivek Manchanda's head. The chalk hit the target and Rajnish glanced at the book on his desk with a serious countenance. He then took the second

LNK Waiting to Settle the Chalk War

one and did a repeat. Then the third and the fourth. Vivek got exasperated and angry. He collected all the chalk pieces, got up and started throwing them in our direction. One chalk hit me and that got me angry because I had not hit him. I also stood up and started hitting back. The noise level in the class went up and as it reached a crescendo, the door opened and LNK walked in looking very upset. Fortunately, the door was in the front of the classroom and Vivek who was still standing and shouting was within striking distance. He got a hard slap for his efforts. LNK then looked at me and told me angrily to come outside the class immediately. I was now ready for the 3rd *thappad* of my tenure in Modern School. As I walked out of the classroom after LNK, I suddenly saw him smile at me. He just said very softly "*Beta, aise kyun karte ho, Kapur saab office mein hain*". He then opened the door and told me angrily to go back to my desk.

There were some unwritten privileges of being a sportsman. I was spared the slap because of this. Many years later when I reminded him of this incident, he smiled and said "*Beta, do you think I should make up now?*"

18

Lunch and Fun Break

The most popular period in the timetable was the lunch break. This was the time to satiate hunger which was built up over 6 academic periods and the milk break. Most of us left for school early in the morning around 7 am after a glass

Lunch with Friends under the Gaze of Kites

of milk or a sandwich. The milk during the milk break was just about enough to quench our thirst. Most of the students waited till the lunch break to dig into the lunch box carried from home. There were other options too. One could buy a 75 ps coupon and join the boarders for lunch in the boarding house mess supervised by Mr. Makhija or pick up a burger or chhole bhature and wash it down with Coke.

It was good to sit with classmates on the huge lawns of the school and have lunch together. One had to watch out for the kites who would swoop to have their share of the food. In winter, sitting out in the sun was a preferred option. In summer, the shade of the trees kept us cool.

The lunch break was not only about food. There was some time for sporting action too. Hand squash was played with gusto next to the old gym (MN Kapur Hall) and other spots where suitable walls were available.

For the students who were not sporty, just catching up with friends regarding the latest movie or music kept them occupied. It was fun time.

19

Mohan Singh Tournament—The Anticlimax

Mohan Singh Memorial Hockey Tournament was organized every year on the Modern School fields. It was named after the founder of Coke bottling franchisee Sardar Mohan Singh and was sponsored and organized by the company. The company had excellent relations with the

Mohan Singh Hockey Final

school since some members of the family were studying there. In fact, an annual visit to the plant located right next to the school campus was organized for the junior students.

Unfortunately, in 1971–72, the tournament was relocated to Shivaji Stadium due to some misunderstanding with the organizing secretary.

This tournament is still fresh in my mind because of the twists and turns in the schedule due to reasons beyond our control. We had a tight schedule. We played 5 matches in 4 days. Our quarterfinal match against Sainik School had to be rescheduled because of rain and we had to play the match the next morning with the semifinal scheduled the same evening. We beat Sainik School 2–0 and then played a tough game against the tournament favourites Daly College, Indore. Rajiv Rastogi and Atul Arora scored a goal each in the first 5 minutes and then we were defending for the next 65 minutes, barring a few runs by the forwards. We finally won 2–1. It was an exhausting game. Next day was the final against St. Joseph School, Meerut.

The final was a tough game. It was evident that St. Joseph had included some overage players from their college team. We decided to play without protest. We lost by 2 goals which we conceded due to defensive errors. Our Principal Mr. Kapur consoled us by saying that we lost unfairly to a team which had overage players who shouldn't have played.

20

The Last Day in School

It is not quite uncommon to note that students will always remember their first day in school. Coping with stress of first day in a new environment is always a challenge for a 4 year old. Similarly, the final day also had certain events which would leave imprint on the student's mind.

On the last day, it was a tradition in the school to not attend classes. While the rest of the school was busy in their respective classes, the graduating batch would spend the day bidding farewell to their teachers and the much respected and loved Principal Kapur. A common practice was to visit the teachers in their classroom and carry them on shoulders on their chair. Normally, the teachers would interrupt the class and allow this ceremonial farewell with good cheer. However, our English teacher and my housemaster Mr. CK Chadha (CKC) had other ideas. He asked the boisterous bunch to come after the period was over. The students were very keen to do it immediately. They rushed into the class and reached for the chair. This infuriated CKC. He snatched the chair and threw it at the students who were now running helter skelter outside the block.

The other tradition was to raid the tuck shop. The owner Mr. Khanna was expecting this and hence offered to host all the students and treated them to a Burger and Coke. The students graciously accepted the offer. It was also customary to put comments and autographs on the friends school uniform—shirts and shorts for boys and kurtas for girls. That

Farewell to Teachers on the Last Day

uniform was preserved by students for posterity as a sign of remembrance.

Parting with friends and classmates of 13 years was always very difficult. There are many memories I cherish even today. It's always a pleasure to go down the memory lane. This book is one such attempt.

21

MNK—The Ultimate Mentor

When I was in the final year of my school in S5, in 1971–72, I was walking down the corridor outside Principal's office, I felt a friendly hand on my shoulders. I looked back to see the smiling countenance of MNK. He wanted to have a word with me. In the next ten minutes, he told me why I will not get the prestigious sports award. I told him I wasn't even

MNK—The Ultimate Mentor

expecting it, the narrow 3rd place finish at the Delhi State Meet had taken care of that. But the significance of the gesture was not lost. I had learnt my first lesson in 'Meritocracy'. Merit was the only criteria. There were no compromises with that principle. It is a value which I cherish even today. More importantly, the bad news was delivered with tremendous sensitivity, grace and dignity.

Almost ten years later, I called him from Bangalore. He was my referee for an assignment at Hindustan Lever Ltd, my dream company. The rigorous selection process was reaching a tense finale. The job would be mine if I got a good reference. 'Off course Sunder, I remember you (not surprising, given his sharp memory), don't worry.' His words were quite reassuring. A month later, I got the offer, a point of inflection in my corporate career. MNK had made a difference.

While these were special moments in my life, MNK touched the lives of all Modernites like no other. When I look at those glorious years, the golden era, some things stand out. It wasn't just about the brick and mortar, the 27 acre campus which made Modern a brand to reckon with. The model for success was a mix of quality of teaching/coaching talent at all levels, a pioneering spirit which took Modern down the path not trodden and above all MNK's inspirational leadership which was the key differentiator. Modern was an institution without peers.

'The Battle of Waterloo was won on the playing fields of Eton and Harrow.' How often did the Modernites of that generation hear this in the morning assembly. While academic excellence was at the core of the agenda, the focus was on all-round excellence. Lessons in leadership and teamwork were not taught in the classrooms, but by putting the students through a series of experiences which honed their skills. His mentorship did not stop with the students. The teachers had a development agenda of their own. Every interaction with MNK was a learning experience. 'Enjoy the treat at Bengali Market' is what he will say to the winning teams. 'Celebrating small wins' is the management jargon in fashion today.

MNK enlisted all the stakeholders—students, teachers and others into founder Lalaji's vision for the school—'Turning little children into good citizens and honorable people'. This was to be achieved through all round development of body, mind and character. He was an inspiring and a forward-looking leader. Men like him leave a legacy which lasts much beyond their lifetime. His impact on students and teachers alike was lifechanging. Today, he lives in the heart of those whose lives he touched.

22

Modern School—The Life Changer

It's not for nothing that the 60s' and 70s' is known as the Golden Era of Modern School. Principals Kamala Bose who was the school's first Principal and subsequently MN Kapur, ably guided by the Founder Lala Raghubir Singh and Board of Trustees (BOT) stayed true to the vision and built the foundation for long term success. It was a school without peers.

The intent was to 'Turn little children into honorable citizens' through a curriculum which went beyond academics. The infrastructure in the heart of Delhi which comprised the facilities for sports, co-curricular and extra-curricular activities was best-in-class. The school was the tops in academics reflected through the Board Exam results. It won 'Nehru Flag', a symbol of supremacy in sports every year since its inception. Our cultural prowess displayed during school and house events was unmatched. The students had a wide range of activities to choose from—Arts, Craft, Clay Modelling, Music, Photography, Radio Engineering, Aero Modelling and many more. On the sports field you could choose any game—Cricket, Football, Hockey, Basketball, Volleyball, Softball, Rugger Touch, Badminton, Table Tennis, Athletics, Swimming, Horse Riding, Tennis, etc. The girls also participated in the events.

I had a slow start as described in the earlier chapters but came into my own in the senior school. The transformation was huge. From a reluctant student, I started enjoying the school. It became a home away from home. I could never imagine I could play so many games and enjoyed batik and 'tie and dye'.

The Life Changing Experience

The housemaster was like a parent in the school. The teachers became my life coaches who would advise me even after I had graduated. They left a deep imprint and made a difference to me which was truly life changing.

The reason for writing this book was to capture some moments of that era. I am sure every Modernite would have gone through similar experiences.

Modern was a school with a vibrant soul which lives within us. It is said that **'You may leave Modern, but Modern will never leave you'.**

My Uncle Mr. AH Hemrajani, My Mentor

Sunder Hemrajani and Ajay Gupta Jointly receiving the Hockey Colours

Sunder Escorting the Chief Guest Mr Dharambir Sinha, Deputy Minister, I&B
along with Housemaster Ashoka House Mr CK Chadha
at the Annual House Function

Sunder, President MSOSA (1998–2000)
with Dr Minoo Shroff (Class of 1938) releasing the MSOSA Sandesh

MSOSA Leadership Lecture Series—McKinsey Worldwide
Chief Rajat Gupta (Class of 1966),
Maj. Gen Virendra Singh (Retd) and Principal RK Bhatia in 1999

MSOSA Leadership Lecture Series—Cabinet Minister Arun Shourie (Class of 1958),
Mrs Ketaki Sood, Chairperson Modern School and Senior Modernites
at Modern School in 2000

My Class of 1972 Buddies and Our Gurus at the Class Reunion—
Friends for Life

Modernites Hockey Team, My Fellow Travellers for
Facilitating Hockey Revival in Modern School

MSOSA Recognition for the Hockey Revival Effort—
Mr Ashok Pratap Singh, President, Board of Trustees did the Honors

Passion for Hockey

Sunder and Akhil—Father and Son Wearing the MSOSA Colours with Pride

With my HBS Guru Prof Ranjay Gulati (Class of 1980)
under the Banayan Tree

Hemrajani Boys under the Iconic Banyan Tree

Hemrajani Boys with Sir Alex Ferguson at HBS—An Inspiration

Recognition by Peers—Ultimate Honour

Sunder, Term Trustee, Board of Trustees and Chairman, Modernites Trust with Principal Dr Vijay Datta at Graduation Ceremony, Class of 2020

Sunder, President MSOSA with Justice Sanjay Kishan Kaul (Class of 1976), Chairman, Modernites Trust—A Perfect Partnership

Honouring Paralympian Sharad Kumar (Class of 2010), Bronze Medallist, Tokyo Olympics

MSOSA Dream Team

2nd Innings

Serving My Alma Mater

23

Interregnum— The Modernite Returns

My association with Modern School has two distinct phases. The first phase was the schooling phase which started in 1959 in KG1 (Nursery) and finished with S5 (11th Class) in 1972.

The Route of Life

The second phase started as an alumnus when I got associated with MSOSA (Modern School Old Students Association) during my stint with HUL as Branch Manager of the company in Delhi.

In between these two stints, I finished my college education, graduation in Mechanical Engineering and post-graduation in Management (MBA). My subsequent corporate career took me through significant stints in Hyderabad where I met my wife Kamala followed by stints in Mumbai, Chennai, Bangalore and Delhi. Along the way, I was blessed with 2 wonderful children Akhil and Rohan in Mumbai and Delhi respectively. The high point was, when Akhil and subsequently Rohan got admission in Modern School in 1992 and 1994 respectively. I was always very keen that they study in Modern. There was also a family situation which had developed during my stay in Delhi. I lost my father in 1991. My mentor, my uncle who had played a significant role in my life was diagnosed with Alzheimer's disease in 1995. I needed to be in Delhi. I had to make a difficult choice. In a career shift, I left HUL to join Whirlpool, a white goods MNC which had its India Headquarters in Delhi. The corporate career included significant tenures with PepsiCo and Times Group.

Since I was now in Delhi, I got sucked into the activities of the alumni association and this brought me back to my school in various assignments. This phase has lasted for over 25 years. The journey continues.

24

Born Again—Repurposing Life

This quote was narrated to me by the current Principal of Modern School Dr Vijay Datta. I had gone to meet him to handover a copy of my first book 'Beyond the Mountains: Overcoming the Challenges Within'. During the formative years, what you learn, comes back to you at conscious and subconscious level. The basic instincts developed during the school tenure help you to take decisions later in your life. The years in school were a defining period for me.

In the early '90s, my destiny took me back to Modern School. In 1991, I arrived in my hometown Delhi. I got involved with MSOSA (Modern School Old Students Association) activities. I was elected as its President from 1998–2000. I was MSOSA nominee on the Modernites Trust, its philanthropic arm from 1996–2008. I was nominated the Chairman of the Trust in 2008 and served in the position till my retirement at the age of 65 years in 2020. Soon after, I was elected as the President of MSOSA again from 2020–2022.

Along the way, I served as a member of the Managing Committee (MC) of Modern School, Barakhamba Road (BKR) and later Modern, Vasant Vihar. Even today, I continue to serve on the MC of Modern BKR.

I was nominated as a 'Term Trustee' of the Modern School Board of Trustees (BOT) in 2019. The BOT guides and provides direction to all the schools under the Modern School Society.

I have always considered these positions as a platform to serve my alma mater. I have been fortunate to do so. It was intuitive to get involved with the school. This is a part of giving back—*gurudakshina*. These opportunities have also helped me repurpose my life with renewed vigour—a commitment to support the institutions which gave me so much besides serving various communities and making a difference to them. Reaching for a high hanging fruit takes effort and commitment.

The feeling was one of renewal and rebirth. I was 'Born Again'.

25

Making a Difference—Empowerment through Education

Any philanthropic agenda requires a long-term commitment to issues which impact various communities. While the Modernites Trust is focused on this agenda, MSOSA has provided continuous support over decades. The MSOSA-Modernites Trust partnership has been critical for its success. The scholarship program has changed the lives of many. Since inception in 1983, there have been over 110 beneficiaries.

It is believed that you can empower communities through education. Over a period of almost 40 years, the Modernites Trust has focussed on this aspect of supporting underprivileged sections of the society.

Scholarship Program

The Modernites Trust which was incorporated in 1983 by senior modernites Late Justice Prakash Narain (class of 1938), Mr. Shashi Puri (class of 1953) and others started with scholarship program. The program was targeted at students who had the potential but were deprived of quality education due to paucity of funds. The Trust selected meritorious but needy students through a transparent selection process. Every year 2 students were selected for admission to S1 (Class VI) at Modern School, BKR. The funds were provided through individual donations and surplus from MSOSA activities. At any point of time there were 14 students (S1–S7) studying under this program.

Own a Scholarship Program

Providing Laptops to Scholars

In 2008, to scale up the program, the Trust decided to reach out to various batches for raising funds within the batch of Modernites and sponsoring scholarships. The response was quite overwhelming. The average intake was increased to 5 students per year. Today, there are 35 students studying in the school under this program. They are sponsored by 8 batches and 12 individuals/entities. The Trust also supports meritorious sportspersons studying in the school for their sports activities. Overall, there have been over 110 beneficiaries under the scholarship program since inception.

Dare to Dream

The objective of the program is to enable the deserving scholars to realise their dreams by supporting them to join professional courses and streams of their choice. This includes support for coaching for admissions to professional institutes for engineering and medicine. This program has already started yielding rich dividends.

The Trust has also scaled up financial support to scholars to pursue their career choices after school. This is also applicable to sportspersons of national standing. It's heartening to note that some scholars who received support from the Trust in the school and are doing well have come back to lend their support to this program thus completing the virtuous cycle.

26

Supporting the Teaching Community

The teachers constitute important stakeholders of the Modern School fraternity. They gave best years of their lives to execute the founder's vision. They played an important role of not only educating generations of Modernites but also mentoring them. The Gurudakshina program was started in 1999 to honour the retired teachers. The award includes an honorarium which over years has been increased from Rs 50,000 to Rs 1,00,000 and a shawl. Every year 3 teachers are selected for this award. Since 2011, the Trustees have decided to give award posthumously to some teachers who had passed away before the award was institutionalised. The citation is received by their families.

The school has a lot to do with what we have achieved in our life. The teachers mentored us and helped us build a solid foundation. Our relationship with them is forever. MSOSA is a part of this community. The Gurupranam initiative was launched in 2018 to support the retired teachers in good times and bad. It enabled the retired teachers to avail the services of Modernite Professionals—Doctors, Lawyers, Chartered Accountants, etc. There was also a corpus set up to help them with medical expenses. During Covid, this facility was extended to the serving teachers for medical expenses incurred beyond the insurance cover. MSOSA also reached out to all Modernites around the world to raise funds for this noble initiative. In any crisis, the citizens must stand up. This is a part of giving back to the community which did so much for us. Over Rs 25 lacs was collected to add to the earlier corpus set up. This will see us through the pandemic and more.

Honoring the Teachers—Justice Sanjay Kishan Kaul (class of 1976) Chairman, Modernites Trust with Dr Vijay Datta, Principal, Modern School

27

MSOSA—Towards Higher Purpose

Modern School Old Students Association (MSOSA) was set up in 1957 with the intent to promote bonding within the old students community and with the students of the school. The first 25 years were devoted to cultural activities to promote the social interaction within these communities.

In 1983, a group of senior Modernites decided to establish 'The Modernites Trust', a philanthropic arm—an outreach to the underprivileged sections of society. The purpose was to get involved in charitable activities, especially education for the students from these sections. This was a defining moment. Since then, most philanthropic activities are undertaken in partnership with the Trust.

To promote its objectives, MSOSA expanded its range of activities to sports, inter-school debates, etc. While there was continuity provided by the Annual Play, the bonding with Modernites was strengthened through Senior Modernites Dinner and 50 yr/30 yr Reunions which brought Modernites of different generations back to the school. The Annual Ball catered to the needs of younger generation of Modernites. The Trust also expanded its domain to reach out to the retired teachers through its programs.

The pandemic provided the most significant challenge to MSOSA since its inception. It disrupted the annual calendar of activities due to various restrictions imposed by the regulatory bodies. The Association moved quickly to adapt to the changed scenario. The physical activities had to be postponed or cancelled. The online format helped us innovate. It leveraged the format to expand the reach and connect with Modernites around the world. *Zoom Dhamaka* and the Theatre Festival Programs were huge successes.

Reorganizing activities was the easy part. The pandemic affected all the school communities represented by Modernites, teachers (serving and retired) and school students. It posed various challenges—medical, social, psychological and financial. The school community lost over 80 Modernites and many teachers and students lost their loved ones. There was distress all around. MSOSA organized an online Prayer Meeting to pray for the departed souls and bring closure to the distraught families. It was important to empathize with all who were affected. MSOSA volunteers called up the retired teachers to check on their well-being. Funds were raised from the Modernites community in partnership with the Modernites Trust to provide relief to the teachers and the students to support them in this difficult time.

The fund raiser for 'Dare to Dream' initiative for Modernites who needed financial support to pursue higher education also received good response. Associations like MSOSA need to be driven by a higher purpose and should step up to support our communities in difficult times.

The Modernites Trust under the leadership of its current Chairman Justice Sanjay Kishan Kaul (class of 1976) and a team of committed Modernites continues to make rapid progress to execute the philanthropic agenda. Justice Kaul is a man of integrity and has been my fellow traveller on this journey for over 20 years. The MSOSA-Modernites Trust partnership is vital for its success in the future.

28

Into the Future—MSOSA Core Values

MSOSA was formally registered as a society in 1967. The Memorandum of Articles (MOA) was quite comprehensive.

However, over a period, MSOSA has faced various other challenges. One of the significant challenges is transparency in its operations. MSOSA is a voluntary organization. All the surplus is deployed for charitable purposes through the Trust. When we raise funds from the Modernites community, we are expected to deploy them with transparency and integrity. It is now felt that MSOSA must institutionalize a set of core values and operate at a higher ethical standard. These values are proposed to be incorporated in the MOA as a preamble.

Integrity

The Association and its members need to conduct all aspects of the work in an honorable way, recognizing there is no right way to do a wrong thing and with personal and professional integrity.

Respect

It entails treating others as you would like to be treated. Treat each other with dignity and not focusing your competitive drive on fellow members.

Teamwork

Members must work for the good of the Association. They should freely offer help and assistance to others and seek it when they need it. They should provide constructive criticism as well as praise and encouragement to fellow members.

MSOSA—Core Values

Empathy

This means understanding or feeling what another person is experiencing from their frame of reference. Ability to imagine how the other person is feeling. MSOSA must empathize with all the communities which it serves.

Over the last 65 years, the Association has evolved into a vibrant entity. It is likely to face many more challenges in years to come. It certainly needs a group of committed Modernites who manage its affairs with integrity and transparency. These values will strengthen it further and add to its credibility with the communities.

29

My Personal Journey—Seeking Happiness and Fulfillment

When I look back at my life this far, I have mixed emotions. As with most people, the growing up years were spent preparing for the life ahead. The focus was on education, not just for me but also for my 3 sisters in a joint family. The family

carried the baggage of partition and started life from scratch. In our family, there was a belief that good education was essential for ultimate empowerment. The foundation for life ahead was built at Modern School. Higher education in engineering and business administration provided the springboard to get a good job which ensured financial security.

Modern School has played an important role in my life. I grew up from an introverted child to a confident student when I graduated. I thought the relationship ended then. I then started chasing my career goals. Destiny brought me back to the school, first as a parent in 1992 and then as a member of MSOSA in 1995.

My involvement at Modern deepened when I got elected as President of MSOSA in 1998. The renovation of the old gym (MN Kapur Hall) brought me in touch with the senior trustees of the school—Chairman of the Board of Trustees, Maj Gen Virendra Singh (Retd) and its energetic Secretary, Mr. Ashok Pratap Singh, Ms. Ketaki Sood (also a senior Modernite) and Ms. Anju Pratap Singh, current Chairperson. Subsequently, the relationship with my alma mater got deeper when I was nominated to the Managing Committee of Modern BKR in 2002 and conducted Vision-Mission Workshops in all the three schools. Nomination to the Modernite Trust as a Trustee and subsequently as its Chairperson in 2008 enabled me to contribute to community outside the school by widening the scope of the scholarship program directed at underprivileged sections of the society.

Being member of Managing Committees of schools has provided me an opportunity to work with the next generation of Life Trustees—Late Mr. Pradeep Virendra Singh, current Honorary Treasurer Ms. Mira Pradeep Singh and current

Honorary Secretary Ms. Ambika Pant. The school has completed its 100 years. I was nominated to the Board of Trustees as a Term Trustee in 2019. I am privileged to be offered these platforms to serve my alma mater. What is particularly heartening is that I never had to lobby for these positions. It is my destiny, hand of God and the trust of the stakeholders which has led me here. The school continues to inspire me today as it did when I was a student.

Apart from Modern, there have been other significant influences in my life. I joined Hindustan Unilever Ltd. in January 1982. The 14 years at HUL were a defining period for my corporate career apart from providing financial security. I got married and had 2 children. This also provided some stability in personal life. In addition, looking after the well-being of four seniors was also a priority since my siblings were not in Delhi. There were several twists and turns in the career, but the values imbibed at HUL helped me cope with those challenges.

I attended Advanced Management Program (AMP) at Harvard Business School in 2011. It re-energized and equipped me professionally and personally for the life ahead. It was clear to me that apart from success at work, support to the family and contribution to the society outside were equally important for leading a fulfilling life.

Re-engagement with my alma mater provided me the platform to give back. It also brought great deal of happiness and fulfillment. People seek happiness by earning more money and creating assets. It was true of me as well. But, at this stage of my life, serving my alma mater makes me happy and making a difference to someone's life brings about a feeling of fulfillment.

Along the way, in the early years of this millennium, I was able to help the school revive the game of hockey. Playing on the school field brought back fond memories of my days in the school and playing with the gen-next school players which included my son Akhil brought tremendous joy. A Modernites versus Modern School game over the weekend became a regular feature. The school started winning the trophies again. The Modernites Sports Day was incorporated in the MSOSA annual calendar.

Destiny has brought me to this point. It's been a journey to cherish. I look forward to the life ahead with optimism.

Carrying on the School's Sporting Tradition—
Annual Modernites Sports Day

30

The Final Word—Still Batting

Writing this book has been an emotional experience. Going down the memory lane has its pitfalls. There are moments of joy and sadness. Life is like that. I went back to the '50s. The family was coming to terms with the difficult period in the aftermath of partition. Uprooted from a home in Sindh (now in Pakistan), train journey to Karachi, followed by a steamer ride to Bombay and finally train to Delhi must have been stressful. In spite of the pain experienced during this period, there were no complaints. There was no dearth of love and affection. The family was content with whatever card destiny had dealt. They worked hard and rebuilt their lives. The values of integrity and respect were imbibed then.

Sending me to Modern School was a well-considered decision. We led a frugal life. Modern School was a huge investment into the future. Looking back, it was the significant step my family took to put me on the road to a fulfilling life. It helped me deal with introversion and become a confident adult. I met some mentors who made a difference to my life and made lifelong friends. These relationships continue even today. The lessons in leadership and teamwork learnt on the playing fields of the school were never forgotten. The learnings stay with you throughout your life and help you cope with challenges on the way.

The second defining moment was joining HUL in 1982. It was a company which had a strong value system. Integrity being the most significant. It reinforced my values imbibed during my upbringing. The company's people-centric approach brought enormous knowledge and financial security. I met some wonderful people who continue to be friends. This also brought me back to Delhi and helped me re-engage with my alma mater Modern School as a parent, and then as an alumnus. The professional journey moved forward in spite of a few bumps along the way. The association with Modern deepened.

Still Batting

In 2006, I started teaching the MBA students at Faculty of Management Studies (FMS), a part of University of Delhi, my alma mater. I was invited as a guest faculty to teach marketing electives. This also brought a realization that I had to update my knowledge. The world of management had moved on since I did my MBA in 1979. I was advised by my friend and mentor Dr Lalit Johri to attend the Advanced Management Program (AMP) at Harvard Business School. I enrolled for the 8 week program and went back to the classroom as a student. It was a point of inflection. It was like drinking from a fire hose. The HBS mission is educating leaders who make a difference in the world. It was not just about academics but about family, community, and life. Leaders must create value for the society before claiming value for themselves.

The following words expressed during my reading on the graduation day at HBS capture the sentiments.

Rebirth

The Shishya (Pupil) sought the Guru (Teacher). The world had changed beyond comprehension since he was born. He wanted to enhance knowledge to cope with the changes. The Guru had seen different worlds. He was eternal. He beckoned the Shishya to the Ashram (Spiritual abode of the Guru). The learning was intense. The Shishya was enlightened by the wisdom accumulated over generations. He was now ready to face the 'new world' and the future with confidence. He was reborn.

Finally, looking back, I must admit all these institutions have had significant influence on me and made me what I am today. If there is one value which defines me, it's integrity. I have led a life of integrity inspite of several challenges along the way. This is unlikely to change.

Footprints

One night I had a dream;
I dreamed I was walking along the beach with God,
And across the sky, flashed scenes from my life.
For each scene, I noticed two sets of footprints in the sand;
One belonged to me, and other to God.

When the last scene of my life flashed before us,
I looked back at the footprints in the sand.
I noticed that many times, along the path of life,
there was only one set of footprints.

I also noticed that it happened at the very
lowest and saddest times in my life.
This really bothered me, and I questioned God about it.
"God, you said that once I decided to follow you,
you would walk with me all the way, but I noticed that
during the most troublesome time in my life,
there is only one set of footprints.
I don't understand why, in times when I needed you most,
you would leave me."

God replied, "My precious, precious child, I love you,
and I would never, never leave you during your times of
trials and suffering.
When you see only one set of footprints,
it was then that I carried you."

CPSIA information can be obtained
at www.ICGtesting.com
Printed in the USA
LVHW052310240522
719627LV00004B/712

9 789390 951277

CPSIA information can be obtained
at www.ICGtesting.com
Printed in the USA
LVHW052310240522
719627LV00004B/712